MONEY AND MARRIAGE

Choices, Rights and Responsibilities

Money and Marriage should be a "must read" for those preparing to marry, as well as those already married. It can help couples prevent money conflicts which undermine many marriages.

Honorable Elizabeth A. Weaver
Justice, Michigan Supreme Court

This book will help many to establish a financially stable and happy family unit and show how proper financial planning can help a marriage to prosper.

Claire Mott White
Grand Blanc, Michigan

We found Jenni's book/class very helpful as we developed guidelines for our financial future together.

Dave and Joy McBride
McBride Construction, Petoskey, Michigan

Ms. Huffman has written a "must" self-help book for families. She has lots of penetrating questions.

Richard E. Olds
Professor of Psychology Emeritus
Millersville University of Pennsylvania

MONEY AND MARRIAGE

Choices, Rights and Responsibilities

A Guide to Financial Compatability for Your Partnership

Jennifer Lee Huffman

MONEY AND MARRIAGE

Choices, Rights and Responsibilities

By Jennifer Lee Huffman

Published by:

Torch Lake Publishing

Post Office Box R

Petoskey MI 49770-0918 USA

+First Printing 1998

Publisher's Cataloging-in-Publication

(Provided by Quality Books, Inc.)

Huffman, Jennifer Lee.
    Money and marriage : choices, rights, and
responsibilities / Jennifer Lee Huffman. —1st ed.
    p. cm.
    Preassigned LCCN: 98-90239
    ISBN: 0-9664232-0-8

    1. Married people–Finance, Personal. 2. Marriage law–
Popular works.   I Title.

HG179.H84 1998   332.024'0655

                                QB198-777

Printed in the United States of America

Table of Contents

Introduction

Money and Marriage: Choices, Rights and Responsibilities was written to help people establish their financial balance and develop their financial self-sufficiency within a marriage. Many control games are power plays perpetuated by the financial practices within a family. It would help most people to know what their financial rights are within the family structure and how to assess their own needs, choices, and values, while allowing all other family members the same freedom to participate in financial decisions. **Use the worksheets in this book to find out your financial compatability with a potential spouse or to set up a useful financial system for your marriage.**

There is no right or wrong way to manage your family and personal finances, but this book will help **create an environment** where choices, decisions, and knowledge can be taught and used by each family member. The ability to define all family members' rights, choices and responsibilities will help the family unit achieve financial goals without using control or domination. Families need to create a financial environment where each member is valued, appreciated, and taught how to be a contributing partner of the family unit, regardless of the financial contribution.

This book was written to help myself and others move through and out of financial dependencies with other people and things. It was designed to help other people develop their own financial self-esteem at the same time they are in a marriage, business, or family partnership of any kind, without having to control or manipulate the situation.

Most long term marriages will go through at least forty-five financial changes. **Money and Marriage** was written after my marriage of twenty-one years ended. Through the years I have learned to adapt to many changing financial situations. Beginning my financial journey as a high school French teacher after graduation from college, marrying and having two incomes without children, I worked while my husband attended law school, and then started a family. During these early years in our marriage, when my husband began his law practice, I learned to adapt to changing financial situations since our family lived on a tight budget. I worked at home with two small boys, returned to college to complete my Masters Degree, ran several small businesses out of our home, and managed the finances for all of these endeavors.

Professionally, I also learned how to adapt to changing financial situations while I was Assistant Director of Financial Aid at GMI Engineering and Management Institute where I dealt with students and their families' unique financial needs. I ventured into the entrepreneurial field when I left my job to have our third son and opened three restaurants in the year following his birth. I also have acted as General Contractor on four of our homes as well as the restaurants.

In addition to a law practice, my husband was adept at finding low-cost real estate properties. We began buying rental homes and real estate which we put into family limited partnerships. I am currently the General Partner of one of them and have managed the finances of all of them at one time or another. When my husband and I opened adult foster care homes, I held the position of Director of Administration and Finance for the corporation.

Personally, I am learning to face new challenges each day as a single mother with two sons in college and the third one in middle school. **I am learning once again how to adapt our financial needs to the changing situations of our individual lives.**

This book is designed to help people become financially self-sufficient, rather than co-dependent. It encourages people to **use money as a tool** to personal growth and satisfaction, rather than as a **method of control and power** over another.

This book is dedicated to all those people who truly wish to have a fair and healthy financial relationship for themselves and their marriage partnership.

Notes:

Chapter One:

Financial Rights in Marriages

The purpose of **Money and Marriage** is to help each family member meet his/her own financial needs by empowering each partner with certain rights, responsibilities, knowledge, and choices regardless of one's financial status in the marriage. Each partner as an individual has financial rights within a partnership. The partnership as an entity of its own, has financial rights, as well. Your individual rights, as well as the rights of the partnership need to be both respected and maintained throughout the marriage. These rights may include:

1. The right to make financial choices.

2. The right to take financial responsibility.

3. The right to gain financial knowledge.

4. The right to give and receive informative answers to financial questions which are legitimately the business of your partnership.

5. The right to have your financial choices and values acknowledged as important to you.

6. The right to have your financial and family re sponsibilities spoken of with respect, whether paid or not.

7. The right to decide together how the **family** finances are managed, earned, distributed and accounted for.

8. The right to decide independently of another, how your **personal** finances are managed, earned, and accounted for.

9. The right to discuss any **family** financial issues free from angry outbursts, physical or emotional threats, and punishments.

10. The right to communicative, sharing, safe, family financial meetings.

11. The right to be financially self-sufficient.

12. The right to live free from financial dictatorship.

13. The right to adapt your financial plans to meet family goals, needs, incomes, and situations.

14. The right, **annually,** to reassess the financial responsibilities and choices of the family members.

15. The right to participation in the financial management, distribution and accounting of family assets.

16. The right to have your contributions to the family welfare appreciated by others regardless of age or position in family.

To make the most out of this book, be willing to design a financial system for yourself and your family which provides for each family member's needs. Be willing to think originally about how to use money. Drop preconceived concepts of using money (or the lack of it), as a power or control over others. Begin with the premise that each individual has the ability to learn sound financial concepts, make his/her own financial choices, and act responsibly toward him or herself, to his/her family, and ultimately to our community and world.

This book may help you recognize and put into practice your own values, goals, and action steps which benefit you, your spouse, and your marriage partnership as a unit. As you learn to start with your values in life, choose other goals and actions which will then support and become the foundation for your values. When your values are set, then you can make the conscious choices which perpetuate those values in all aspects of your life.

Values are the qualities of life you hold in esteem and choose to emulate in yourself and your family.

Goals are your conscious choices and commitments which lead to and become the self-perpetuating foundations of your values.

Your daily and weekly **tasks**, activities, and steps are the actual building blocks for attaining your goals. Become aware of some basic values and rights in financial partnerships in order to design a system which benefits **each family member.**

Notes:

Chapter Two:

General Format/Structure

The chapters on **Knowledge, Choices,** and **Responsibilities** will instruct and lead you through a series of exercises and worksheets. They are designed to make you aware of your financial values, gain financial knowledge, make your own choices and take responsibility for your financial goals and commitments. At the same time, the chapters may help you create an environment wherein your partner can choose to achieve his/her individual and family financial goals at the same time.

Prepare a three ring notebook for **each** of the adults and **one** for the family as a whole. Each adult notebook needs section dividers with these headings:

1. Knowledge/Rights

2. Goals

3. Reading Notes

4. Debts

5. Choices

6. Responsibilities

Your own adult notebook is your own personal possession and need not be shared with anyone, for you also have a right to privacy for your own goals and plans.

By the end of the book, you will have completed many different worksheets. Some are to be inserted in your personal adult financial notebook as instructed upon completion, while the rest are to be put in the family financial notebook.

Annually, you will be revising most of the worksheets in your own financial notebook. It is vital for you to **assess** your rights, choices, status, goals, and your family situation on an annual basis. Our families are in a constant state of financial flux.

The family which knows how to adapt to the financial changes of the marriage will provide a secure foundation for each family member.

The notebook designated for family use is called the **Family Financial Notebook.** It needs sections with these headings:

1. Concerns

2. Ideas

3. Decisions

4. Family Meetings

5. Annual Budgets

6. Monthly Budgets

The Family Financial Notebook is to be used for all meetings, budgets, and summaries of family financial issues. It should be **available to everyone in the family at any time.** Family finances are to be shared with everyone with daily opportunities for information gathering and questions. Healthy families cultivate environments where both openness and privacy are provided to all members, but not secrecy or control.

Balancing your responsibility for contributions to the family welfare and your need for autonomy is one of your main goals.

In a secure family, each person contributes to the family, financially or in other non-money ways, and yet is accorded the rights of spending money, taking responsibility, making choices, setting goals, and gaining knowledge in the financial area without anyone else telling him/her what to do.

This book is designed to help you communicate with other family members and to help you learn about your own values and needs. Please do all the exercises in the order given, ask each family member if he/she would like to do them, and don't quit when you realize how unique and different everyone else is. Some of the exercises may be simplistic, but do them anyway. Some of the worksheets may be difficult, but do them anyway.

A financial partnership is an on-going adaptive process which requires growth, original thinking and acting to provide a financial system which is **beneficial to everyone in your family**. If your spouse chooses not to do the exercises, then do the worksheets on your own. You need to take responsibility for your own financial rights, responsibilities, choices and knowledge, **regardless of those around you.**

Notes:

Chapter Three:

Knowledge of My Own Financial Needs and Values.

There are three kinds of knowledge you need to acquire in order to be successful in developing a healthy family financial system where each member's rights, choices, and responsibilities are honored.

1. Awareness of your **own** financial values, rights, and choices,

2. Awareness of **other** family members' rights, values and choices,

3. Knowledge of and skill with sound basic financial concepts.

The following exercises are designed to help you and your family members find out what *each one's needs and values* are in a rational way. Since most people need to **learn** how to listen and understand other people's views, there are also specific exercises designed to help you communicate and share your needs and ideas to your family members and to enable them to show you what their needs and values are.

In addition, it is important to have this information **communicated in a safe environment** where sharing is encouraged, accepted and demanded as the **foundation** for all future learning and decision making.

The end result of this participation may be:

1) increased self-esteem for all family members (not just the main breadwinners),

2) knowledge and respect for what it really takes to provide for a family and oneself,

3) communication skills so needed in families and society,

4) value as a family member no matter what the age or financial contribution, and

5) the ability to openly discuss important financial issues within a family without being put down, abused or ignored.

Note:

Be honest in your responses to the questions. Be yourself, answer truthfully, and it will be much easier to design your own financial system. You are just gathering information and knowledge about yourself so you can use it for a constructive purpose. Therefore, do not second guess or self-judge yourself during any of these exercises.

If your spouse chooses to read this book, he/she will be instructed to ask for or do specific tasks at certain times, just as you are. **Take responsibility for your own actions,** not your spouse's.

Worksheet One:
Where are You?

Are you aware of the different financial stages your marriage may go through, whether you are presently single, engaged, married for one year or fifty, divorced, or widowed?

Are you willing to make financial decisions and choices together each year as partners at each stage of financial change? Where are you now?

Write in a yes or no after each statement.

1. *Do you believe marriage is a:*
    * *legal partnership*
    * *moral partnership*
    * *physical partnership*
    * *financial partnership*
    * *emotional partnership*
    * *spiritual partnership*
    * *piece of paper*
    * *sacred covenant*
    * *love affair*
    * *trap*

- *something for others*
- *journey to your wholeness*
- *journey to someone else's wholeness*
- *way to have your needs met*
- *way to have someone else's needs met*
- *the safest way to raise children*
- *an institution which stabilizes society*
- *commitment to your individuality*
- *commitment to spouse's individuality*
- *commitment to partnership as a whole*
- *equality in value for each partner*
- *one spouse is head over the other*
- *an historical tradition in most civilizations*
- *two half people becoming one person*
- *two whole people joining together*

2. How many answers were the same as your spouse?

3. What is your best description of a marriage:

4. How many of the following financial stages have you already experienced?

- *Single, working outside home, but living with a parent,*
- *Single, working outside home, living in own place,*

• *Engaged, working outside home, but living with a parent,*

• *Engaged, working outside home, but living in own place,*

• *Engaged, working outside home, living together with fiance,*

• *Married, one working outside home, one inside home,*

• *Married, one working outside home, one inside home with one or more children at home,*

• *Married, one working outside home, one attending school or college,*

• *Married, one working outside home, one attending school or college, with children at home,*

• *Married, both working outside home,*

• *Married, both working outside home with children at home,*

• *Married, both working outside home, children at home, one or more attending college,*

• *Married, both working outside home, no children at home, but one or more children attending college,*

• *Married, both working outside home, both spouses attending school,*

• *Married, neither working outside home, both attending school,*

• *Married, neither working outside home, both attending school, children at home,*

• *Divorced, working outside home,*

- *Divorced, working outside home with children at home,*

- *Divorced, working in home with children at home,*

- *Divorced, attending school, working outside home,*

- *Divorced, attending school, working outside home with children at home,*

- *Retired, one still working outside home,*

- *Retired, one still working inside home,*

- *Both retired,*

- *Both retired with care of dependent,*

- *Widowed,*

- *Widowed with care of dependent,*

- *Retired with care of ill spouse,*

- *Married, working outside of home with care of ill spouse and/or children.*

5. Now, how many more options can you add to the complete list above to see how many different financial changes your marriage may encounter.

Extra Options:

- *Remarriage*

- *Care of parent*

- *Children's college expenses*

- *Start up of a business*
- *Bankruptcy of a business*
- *Sudden job loss*
- *Extended job loss*
- *Child support*
- *Spousal support*
- *Inheritance*
- *Gifts*
- *Lottery*
- *Death of income-producing spouse*
- *Loss of savings*
- *Addictive habits*

6. *Ask yourself, if I am just beginning a marriage or am in the middle of one, how many total situations might I still go through?*

7. *Are you and your spouse equipped financially to handle each of these changing financial stages?*

8. *Are you and your spouse equipped emotionally to handle each of these changing stages?*

9. *Add up the number of different financial stages which you can see as possible for you. Write in the number here.*

Worksheet Two:
Understand Yourself

Answer these questions with a yes or no response.

1. Do you need a safe way to talk about finances with your spouse?

2. Do you know what financial skills you or your spouse need to survive on your own?

3. Do you know what financial skills your children need to survive on their own?

4. Does your family know how to make intelligent financial decisions which benefit all family members?

5. Do you and your spouse have a method for deciding who spends, earns, and pays out money for common family bills?

6. Do you and your spouse have a method for deciding who spends, earns, and pays out money for your personal money choices?

7. Do you have an equal voice in the financial management of your household?

8. If you do not have equal say in your family financial system, what percent would describe it?

9. Do you know how to find out what your spouse really thinks about certain financial choices and values?

10. Do you know how to disagree with your spouse about money without losing your temper or becoming totally frustrated?

11. Do you know how to disagree with your spouse about money without fear of punishment, rejection or anger on their part?

12. Are your children able to talk with you about money in a safe environment?

13. Does your spouse know how to disagree with you about money without fear of rejection, punishment, or anger from you?

14. Are you willing to set up a family financial system which benefits each family member?

15. Do you value each family member as a person with rights, choices, and responsibilities within your family unit?

16. Has a family member less value because he/she is a baby, teen-ager, elderly parent, a debilitating illness, a student, working at home, taking care of children full-time, or working outside the home?

17. Do you equate worth for your spouse only if he/she is an income-producing partner?

18. Have you ever thought about these types of questions?

Add up the number of "yes" answers for questions 1 through 15. If you have 12 or more, "wow, I want to live in your family!" If you have 8 to 11 "yes" answers, then your family is doing okay. If you have less than 8 "yes" answers, your family needs to learn financial communication skills and choices now!

Worksheet Three:
Million Dollar/Time Decisions

If it was only up to me, what would I do with a million dollar gift?

	Amount	Items
For Myself:	_____	
For Spouse:	_____	
For Children:	_____	
For Parents:	_____	
For Business:	_____	
For Charity:	_____	
For Community:	_____	
For World:	_____	
For Savings	_____	
For Investments	_____	
For Friends	_____	
Other:	_____	

$1,000,000.00 Total Amount Spent

During the course of a month, how would I use my time if I were financially independent.....

Amount of Time

For me: _____

With spouse: _____

With children: _____

With parents: _____

With business: _____

With charity/volunteer: _____

For community: _____

For world: _____

For investments/financial: _____

With friends: _____

Other: _____

Total Hours per Month _____

Worksheet Four:
Financial Skills Checklist

Put a checkmark next to each skill you currently practice. Do not put a checkmark if any other person does it for you, even if you know how to do the task.

1. Write checks

2. Maintain the balance in the checkbook

3. Make bank deposits

4. Reconcile the checkbook when bank statement comes from the bank

5. Have filing system for receipts and cancelled checks

6. Make up monthly summary of money spent and income earned

7. Keep budget book or daily expense record of money spent

8. Have regular monthly finance meetings with spouse/family

9. Set and write down financial goals

10. Purchase own clothes

11. Pay bills and tips at restaurant

12. Have own spending money/allowance

13. Organize family schedules/activities

14. *Maintain own savings account*

15. *Obtain and pay for auto insurance*

16. *Maintain own checking account*

17. *Prepare own taxes*

18. *Am employed by someone else*

19. *Am self-employed*

20. *Purchase most of family necessities*

21. *Pay fair share of common family expenses*

22. *Purchase/maintain stocks/bonds in own name*

23. *Purchase auto, house, or land in own name*

24. *Make business investments in own name*

25. *Purchase auto, house, or land on behalf of family*

26. *Make business investments on behalf of family*

27. *Prepare financial records for tax preparer*

28. *Purchase groceries for family*

29. *Purchase gifts for family and friends*

30. *Maintain credit card in own name with zero monthly balance*

31. *Apply for a loan in own name*

32. *Pay monthly loan amounts and then pay off early*

33. *Maintain credit card in family name with zero balance*

34. Prepare annual net worth statement for self and family

35. Conduct family financial board meetings

36. Give clear and informative answers to financial questions from family members

These are basic financial skills and responsibilities for living in our world today. These skills are also basic requirements for achieving self-sufficiency and self-esteem whether you are single or a member of a family.

If you put a check mark next to twenty-five or more skills for yourself, then you are taking responsibility for being financially self-sufficient. If you are not participating in or initiating at least 25 of these skills, you may be financially co-dependent.

This book is an advocate of learning to take responsibility for anything you can do on your own and not relying on others to do it for you. The knowledge that you are not dependent on someone for your financial survival enables you to contribute to yourself, your family, and appreciate what it does for you.

Go back to this list and write each family member's name next to each skill he/she practices. Include your spouse (prospective spouse) and all children living at home. One of your family responsibilities is to help create an environment where each family member can grow into a whole person, financially, emotionally, physically, and spiritually.

Since this book is a financial one, it may help show you how to do this for yourself and your family in the financial area.

Your marriage is a life-long partnership which may take you both through many phases of financial situations. Each family member, regardless of financial contribution to the family, has the right to learn how to be financially self-sufficient, not co-dependent. Your responsibility as a spouse is to provide an financial environment which empowers each partner with autonomy, responsibility, knowledge, and choices.

Worksheet Five:
Family Financial Information

For Wife:

Home Address:

Home Phone:

Home Fax:

Work Address:

Work Phone:

Work Fax:

Mobile Phone #:

Voice Mail #:

Social Security #:

Driver's License #:

Passport #:

Blood Type:

Birthdate:

Other Data:

For Husband:

Home Address:

Home Phone:
Home Fax:
Work Address:

Work Phone:
Work Fax:
Mobile Phone #:
Voice Mail #:
Social Security #:
Driver's License #:
Passport #:
Blood Type:
Birthdate:
Other Data:

Children

Names/Birthdate/Social Security#

1.

2.

3.

4.

5.

Step-Children

Names/Birthdate/SS Number

1.

2.

3.

4.

5.

Grand-Parents
Names/Birthdate/Address/Phone

1.

2.

3.

4.

Family Accounts:
Bank:

   Checking Account #:

   Savings Account #:

   Safety Deposit Box::

   Key Location:

Charge Card Numbers:

Visa

Mastercard

Discover

American Express

Other

Location of Important Papers:

Adoption Papers

Estate Plan

Will

Trust Documents

Marriage Certificates

Divorce Judgment

Death Certificates

Birth Certificates

Insurance Policy Numbers and Company:
Auto:

Home:

Life:

Medical:

Prior Year Tax Forms

Retirement Fund Information
1.
2.
3.

Household Inventory
Vacation Home Inventory
Automobile Titles
Passports
Social Security Cards
Titles/Deeds to Land/Home
Land Contracts

Mortgages

Contracts

Veteran's Papers

Bond and Stock Certificates

Notes:

Other Family Information:

Tax Preparer name and phone number:

Attorney name and phone number:

Family Dentist and phone number:

Family Doctor and phone number:

Home Insurance Agent and number:

Life Insurance Agent and number:

Investment Advisor name and number:

Family Vehicles/Boats   *License #*

1.

2.

3.

4.

5.

6.

Ex-Spouse Name

Address

Phone #

Social Security #

Children's Spouses' Names/Address/Phone#

1.

2.

3.

4.

Other Family Homes/Properties/Address/Phone#

1.

2.

3.

4.

5.

Any Other Asset/Property/Vehicles owned with another relative outside of immediate family:

Item   _Name of Relative_

1.

2.

3.

4.

5.

6.

Family Investments: *Type:*

1.

2.

3.

4.

5.

6.

7.

Worksheet Six:
Family Active File

Indicate who is currently responsible for filing and maintaining records for these financial items:

	Location	_Person_
Tax Receipts		
Bank Statements		
Cancelled Checks		
Income Tax Papers		
Unpaid Bills		
Paid Bill Receipts		
Employment Records		
Health Benefit Records		
Credit Card Information		

Life Insurance Policies

Appliance Manuals, Warranties

Mortgage Loan Payment Books

Auto Loan Payment Books

Receipts for Charge Card Items

Child Expenses

Grocery Expenses

Education Expenses

Worksheet Seven:
Personal Records

Complete your personal information sheet for all financial assets **not** in the family name or possession.

Your Name:
Home Address:

Home Phone:
Home Fax:

Work Address:

Work Phone:
Work Fax:
Mobile Phone #:
Voice Mail #:
Birthdate:
Social Security #:
Driver's License #:
Passport #:
Blood Type:
Other:

Personal Accounts:

    Bank:

    My Own Checking Account Number:

    My Own Savings Account Number:

    My Own Safety Deposit Box:

    Key Location:

Investments in my name only:

    1.

    2.

    3.

    4.

Charge Cards in my name only:

1.

2.

3.

4.

Land/Property in my name only:

1.

2.

3.

4.

5.

<u>*Vehicles/Boats in my name only:*</u>

1.

2.

3.

4.

5.

6.

Any Other Assets in my name only:

1.

2.

3.

4.

5.

Location of Important Papers in my name only:

Land

Buildings

Automobile Titles

Insurance Policies

Will

Any Assets in my name and with someone other than a relative:

Note:

The **family** financial information is to be completed, copied, and then put in the family notebook. The worksheet containing **your personal** information does **not** have to be shared with anyone. If you are comfortable giving a copy to your spouse, please do so. If not, then put a copy of the personal sheet in a sealed envelope and leave it somewhere it can be obtained by your spouse in the event of death.

In some cases, this information would be left with your attorney, but your spouse still needs written instructions for where to find out this information. Since you will be reviewing and updating this information annually, you will need to replace your spouse's copy each year.

I encourage you to have complete disclosure with your spouse. The information and openess you choose to give your spouse may result in much greater trust and honesty throughout the marriage.

Worksheet Eight:
Childhood Financial Inventory

Growing up, did you......?

   1. ...get an allowance?

   ...If yes, did you save it?

   ...spend it at will?

   ...follow parental guidelines?

   ...account for where it went?

   ...spend it on what you picked?

   ...spend it on parents' choices?

   ...give any of it away?

   ...lose any of it?

   *...receive it in exchange
      for work?*

   ...Other

   2. ...earn money up to age 14?

   ...If yes, did you save it?

   ...spend it at will?

...follow parental guidelines?

...account for where it went?

..spend it on what you chose?

...spend it on what your parents chose?

...give any of it away?

...lose any of it?

...receive it in exchange for work?

...give any of it to family to use for bills?

...work more than 20 hours per week to earn it?

3....have to work before age 14 but received no cash or paycheck?

...at home?

...how many hours per week?

...in a family business?

...for anyone else?

4. Through age 14 ...

...did you think of your family as poor, average, or well-off?

...did you even care or think about money?

...were you included in any financial discussions or decisions with your parents?

...were you aware of what your family expenses cost?

...did you ever steal any money?

    - from family members?

    - from other people?

    - from businesses?

...did you give it back?

...did you pay it back?

...did you tell anyone?

Other concerns at this age:

5. Did you earn money between the ages of 15 and 18?

...At home?

...In a family business?

...In an outside business?

...Did you save any of it?

...What did you save for?

...Did you ever buy anything completely with your <u>earned</u> money?

...Did you ever buy anything with gift money?

...Did you have your own savings account?

...Could you deposit/withdraw money at will?

...Did you have a checking account?

...Did you balance it each month?

...Who taught you how to balance and use checks?

...Did you do your own taxes?

...Did you have to give any of your earned money to your family?

...How did you know how much you could spend?

...Did you pay for your own clothes?

..Did you pay for your own entertainment (movies, going out, etc.)?

...Did you ever just blow some of your money on someone or something?

...How much? _____

...More than once?

...Did you ever give money away to people?

...For contributions?

...Did you ever lend your money to people?

...Did they always pay you back?

...Did you follow any parental guidelines for using your money?

...Did you account to anyone for where it went?

...Did you track your spending?

Other concerns:

6. Through age 19 ...

...did you think of your family as poor, average, or well-off?

...were you included in family financial discussions or

decisions?

...were you aware of how much your family spent on house, car payments, food, or telephone?

7. From age 19-22 ...

...did you earn money?

...did you receive gift money?

...was your primary occupation student, full-time employee, business owner or other?

...did you attend college full-time?

> *part-time?*

...if yes, who paid for tuition?

> *room/board?*

> *books?*

> *clothing?*

> *spending money?*

...did you earn money to pay for your portion of school responsibilities?

...how did you earn it?

...did you have to work during school or summers to earn money?

...did your parents talk with you about what you were responsible for?

...did you find your own job?

...how did you know who would pay for what at college?

...did you have to account to anyone for spending in any of the five college categories?

...to whom and for which ones?

...did you work full time?

...did you pay for your own:

> *rent?*
>
> *utilities?*
>
> *insurance?*
>
> *car?*
>
> *clothing?*
>
> *food?*
>
> *spending money?*

If you did not pay for these expenses, write down who did.

...did you have to get permission from your parents to get a job? to get an apartment?

...did your parents support you temporarily by paying for any of these items or by allowing you to live at home or use their car and food?

8. **During this age span, or before, did you become a parent or become responsible for the primary welfare of another person?**

9. **Did you marry during this age span or before?**

10. *If you could redo the age 19-22, would you have changed anything in the financial area?*

   ...Did you view yourself as poor, average, well-to-do during this age span?

11. *When you were young, did only the money earner get to distribute money to other family members?*

   ...if yes, did he/she get to decide how to spend it?

   ...if yes, did he/she write out and pay the bills?

   Did one of your parents have to hide or stash money from the other for any reason?

12. *Do you think the use of your income is totally your own choice to earn, spend, give away or waste if:*

   ...single?

   ...married and both working full time?

   ...married w/children and both are working full-time?

   ...married w/children and only you are working out of the home?

13. *Do you need a safe way to talk about finances with your spouse?*

14. Do you know how to agree/disagree with your spouse or family members on financial matters?

15. Have you ever discussed the numerous potential marital financial situations with your fiance or spouse?

16. Write down any other financial issue or circumstance you may have had growing up which adds more to your self-inventory and awareness.

Set up an appointment within the next two days with your spouse in order to share the information from all the worksheets completed to date except your personal financial information sheet. Your spouse has the responsibility to request an appointment with you after he/she is done. Do not do it for him/her. Take care of your own responsibilities. Continue on even if he/she no longer participates.

After the appointments, insert these worksheets into your adult notebook under the Knowledge section.

Share your completed worksheets except for the personal information one. Set aside two hours to do this sharing. Begin by reading the following statement to the listening person.

"I am beginning a new task of taking responsibility for the financial area of my life. My first task was to answer questions about how I would use my time and money, how many financial situations I have been in, and how money was used by me and my family as I was growing up. I would like to share this information with you. I'm looking forward to the time when you share your information with me.

Knowledge of myself and you is one of the first steps to help us create an original family financial plan. First, I would like you to read my answers to these worksheets.

Afterward, if you would like to ask questions to further understand what I wrote down, please do it at that time.

No statements, clichés, put-downs or snickers are to be made during this process, but additional questions by you are welcome. Thank you for taking the time to learn more about me."

Give the listener the worksheets to read. Answer any questions your spouse might have after he/she has finished reading and thank him/her for learning about you.

Worksheet Nine:
Sharing Comfort Level

Complete the following self-analysis by yourself. Answer YES or NO.

...*I felt comfortable during the whole process.*

...*It was easy to do.*

...*I had no problem sharing this information.*

...*It was so simple, it was almost dumb.*

...*I resented having to do this.*

...*It was easy for me to do the inventory, but hard to share it.*

...*It was hard for me to do the inventory, but easy to share it.*

...*It was hard to do both.*

...*Did your listener agree easily to the appointment?*

...*Did the listener make any value judgments or remarks before you read the opening statement?*

...*Did the listener follow the directions and read it to himself/herself first?*

...*Did the listener ask any questions? Make any statements? Say anything you might consider a put-down?*

...*Do you think it was hard for the listener to hear all this information?*

...Do you think he/she learned something new about you?

...When you finished, was there tension between you?

...Did you feel relaxed and satisfied when you finished?

...Did you feel safe sharing this kind of information?

...Did you wonder how the listener was going to react to this exercise?

...Overall, did it go better or worse than you expected?

Completed by: _____

*Date:*_____

Note:

You will use this Worksheet after each communication session with your spouse. Become aware of your feelings and instincts which tell you how the communication process is working.

Put this in your adult notebook under the knowledge section.

Worksheet Ten:
Adult Financial Inventory

This self-inventory is for your use only. Honestly answer these questions regarding your current situation (including the last three years).

1. *Do you receive money/income in your own name?*

2. *Do you earn money by paycheck?*

   ...by investment?

   ...from your own business?

3. *Are you dependent on anyone else for more than half of your current overall financial status?*

4. *Are you contributing financially to more than half of anyone else's total income?*

5a. *Are you dependent on anyone else for providing more than half of the child care to your children?*

5b. Do you pay this person for this type of contribution?

5c. Does your spouse provide more than half of the time necessary to provide for the non-financial necessities of your family? (Like cooking, cleaning, shopping, etc.)

5d. Do you work at a job outside the home for more than 60 hours per week?

6. Do you have any dependents?

7. Do you have regular financial meetings with your spouse and/or children?

8. Do you pay most of the family bills?

9. Do you have a checking account in your name only?

10. Do you have a charge card in your name only?

11. Do you have any assets like a car, house or property in your name only?

12. Would you feel offended or threatened if your spouse wanted his/her own checking account?

...own charge card?

...own major asset ?

...car, house, property?

13. *Would you like to have a checking account, charge card or major asset in your name only?*

14. *Do any of your minor children have a checking account, car, charge card or other major asset in their name only?*

15. *Would you feel offended or threatened if they wanted these in their own names?*

16. *From memory or by guessing, insert dollar amounts you and your family spend on each category per month into the first column of blanks. Leave the second column blank for now.*

Mortgage or rent _____ _____

Utilities/telephone _____ _____

Property taxes and insurance _____ _____

Auto payment and insurance _____ _____

Gas _____ _____

Groceries _____ _____

TOTAL _____ _____

17. From your records, insert dollar amounts spent in each of these areas per month.

Personal & Clothes	Fun & Entertain- ment	Business & Investment	Volunteer & Charity

You:

Spouse:

Kids:

18. Go back to numbers 16 and 17 and put an X mark next to any item for which you have to get approval or money from someone else in order to spend it on that item. If your spouse needs to get either approval or money from you to spend it on an item, put and asterisk (*) next to it.

*19. From your records and calendars, insert
how many hours are spent in each of
these areas per month.*

Personal Growth	*Recreation & Entertain.*	*Volunteer & Charity*

You:

Spouse:

Kids:

*20. Go back to #19 and put an X mark
next to any item for which you have to
get approval or money from someone else
in order to do it. If your spouse needs to
get either money or approval from you to
do it, put an asterisk (*) next to it.*

*21. Go back now to #16 and insert true
spending amounts in the second column
of blanks from your own research. Do not
ask a spouse or friend to do this for you,
but find out for yourself by analyzing the
checkbook, budget book, etc.*

If you do not pay these bills yourself, you may ask your spouse where this information is located, but do the rest yourself. It is your own responsibility. Total the columns and write out the difference you were off at the bottom. If you were more than $100.00 off, mark an asterisk (*) by the amount. If you were less than $100.00 off, put a Y next to it.

22. *Go back now to #16 and 17. If your total monthly dollar amount is more than one-third of your spouse's total amount, make an X mark next to your total monthly amount.*

23. *Go back to #19 and 20. For any line item with less than 10 hours per month, put an asterisk (*) next to it. If your hourly spending total is more than one-third of your spouse's monthly total, make an X mark next to your total.*

24. *Put this in your adult notebook when you are done with the next worksheet.*

Worksheet Eleven:
Adult Inventory Analysis

The numbers for the questions on Worksheet #10 correspond with the **same** numbers on this worksheet. If your answer was YES for that number, then circle the Y and underline the sentence(s) after it.

If your answer was NO, circle the N and underline the sentence(s) after it. If your answer included an *, circle it and underline the sentence after it. If your answer included an X mark, circle it and underline the sentence after it.

Note:

The purpose of this adult inventory is to provide you with knowledge about yourself and your family. It may show you what areas you need to work on, where some of your strengths are, where you are controlling others or allowing yourself to be controlled, and where you either already have or need to take more responsibility in your financial situation.

This analysis is **not** an attempt to prove you are right or wrong in how you manage and communicate your financial affairs.

It is simply to be used as one of your tools for taking charge of your financial affairs, while providing other family members with the same opportunities.

This worksheet is not to be shared with your spouse or family.

1. N= I need knowledge of how to receive money in my own name and I need the responsibility of receiving money in my own name.

Y= I have the responsibility of receiving money in my own name.

2. N= I need knowledge of how to earn my own money.

Y= I have the responsibility of earning this income.

3. N= I have choices in regard to my financial status and I have the main responsibility in providing for myself.

Y= I need to develop more choices in regard to my financial status and I need more responsibility in providing for myself.

4. Y= He/she needs knowledge of the extent of my contribution and he/she needs choices in spending and directing it. I have the main responsibility for financially providing for someone else.

5a. Y= I need knowledge of how he/she is contributing by doing more child care myself and he/she needs more choices for time off and how to spend it.

N= I have the main responsibility of providing care for our children.

5b. *N= I need knowledge of how much this would cost if I had to hire an outsider and I need to take more responsibility for paying my spouse in some form of remuneration. He/she needs some kind of choices and remuneration.*

5c. *Y= I have knowledge of how much time and effort he/she spends and I need to take more responsibility for the direct care of my family.*

N= I need to provide myself with more time off choices.

5d. *Y= I need more knowledge about everything that is happening in my spouse's and children's lives and I need to provide myself with more time off choices.*

6. *N= I need knowledge about the time and financial commitments of having a family. I have many choices for free time and spending money.*

Y= I have the responsibility for raising a family.

7. *N= I need the knowledge of how and when to communicate with my family about money.*

Y= I have the knowledge of what it takes to get everyone communicating about money. I have the responsibility for having regular financial discussions and meetings with my family or spouse.

8. *N= I need knowledge of knowing how to pay bills. I need the responsibility of paying for some of the family bills.*

   Y= I have knowledge of how to pay bills.

9. *N= I need knowledge of how to get an account in my own name. I need the choice of having my own account.*

   Y= I have the choice and responsibility of having an account in my own name.

10. *N= I need the choice of having my own charge card. I need the responsibility of having my own charge card.*

    Y= I have the choice and responsibility of having my own charge card.

11. *N= I need the knowledge, choice, and responsibility of having an asset in my name.*

    Y= I have the choice and responsibility of having an asset in my name only.

12. Y= I need knowledge of how rewarding it is to for a valued partner to have the choice to manage something in one's own name.

13. N= I need the knowledge of how rewarding it is to have and manage something in my own name.

Y= I have the choice to get a charge card, ac count, or asset in my name. I need to take the responsibility for managing my own account or charge card.

14. N= I need knowledge of how a charge card, checking account, etc. could teach responsibility and good judgment to a teenager.

15. Y= I need knowledge of how they could do this responsibly.

N= I have the knowledge of how it is possible for a teenager to manage his/her own credit card/account.

16. N= I need more accurate knowledge of where our money is going. I need the responsibility of tracking our money to see where we spend it.

Y= I have accurate knowledge of where our money is spent. I have the responsibility of tracking our spending patterns.

17/18. X= *I need to be able to choose for myself in these areas.*

*= *He/she needs to be able to choose in these areas. He/she needs to have the choice of using more money to spend on these areas.*

*= *I need to be able to choose in these areas.*

X= *I have the choice of how to spend money in these areas.*

19/20.   a. X= *I need the choice of spending more time in these areas.*

b.*= *He/she needs the choice of spending more time in these areas.*

c. X= *I need to take the responsibility of spending more time in these areas.*

d. *= *He/she needs to take the responsibility of spending more time in these areas.*

e. *= *They need to make their own choices of time spent in these areas with your guidance.*

f. X= *I have many choices in spending my time in these areas.*

*= *He/she needs the choice of spending more time in these areas.*

Congratulations! You have just completed one of the reviews of your financial strengths and problem areas.

When you underlined, "I have", you can certainly feel capable and secure knowing you are able to handle these tasks. When you underlined "I need", you can use it positively to help set goals for yourself and grow toward them.

Do not think that you are incapable of handling those "need" tasks. The great thing about finances is that everyone can learn to do them well, with just a little practice, guidance, and knowledge.

Worksheet Twelve:
Knowledge/Choice Goals

Write in each "I need knowledge" or "I need choices" statement you underlined in WS 11. Write in at least two or three action steps per goal.

1.

2.

3.

4.

5.

6.

7.

Worksheet Thirteen:
Responsibility Goals

Write in each "I need responsibility" statement that you underlined. Then write in 2 or 3 action steps you could take to move toward that goal.

1.

2.

3.

4.

5.

6.

7.

Worksheet Fourteen: Skill Goals

Write down each financial skill from worksheet #4 which you do not currently practice. Then write in 4 or 5 action steps you could take to move toward that skill.

1.

2.

3.

4.

5.

6.

7.

Worksheet Fifteen:
Financial Goals for Others

Write down all underlined sentences which started with "He/she needs knowledge". Then list three specific things (for each one) that you could do to help your spouse. Do the same for the **Choice** section.

Knowledge:

1.

2.

3.

4.

5.

Choice:

1.

2.

3.

4.

5

Worksheet #15 is not to be shared with your spouse or family. Your goal is to find ways to help your spouse grow in these areas by giving your encouragement, time, and acceptance of his/her choices. There is no responsibility sheet here because it is not up to you to make your spouse take on more responsibilities. Your job is to provide a safe and encouraging environment in which he/she can grow, as well as yourself.

It is your responsibility to help yourself grow with or without your spouse's help. Copy the goals from each of these four worksheets onto a 3x5 card. Put it in your wallet to look at and act upon each day.

Chapter Four:

Knowledge of Others' Financial Values

You have just worked your way through a number of exercises to help you understand what your own financial values, beliefs and conditions are. If your spouse has been participating, you may have learned about his/her financial past.

At this point in time, most of the knowledge you have been **gathering is about you and from your point of view.** A real challenge may come when you learn to listen to your spouse's information about what he/she wants and needs. It may be difficult as you learn to respond in such a way which **provides for his/her progress and growth, as well as your own.**

Awareness of your other family members' rights, goals, values and information is gained through certain **listening skills** which most of us need to learn. You will continue to use more worksheets to become aware of your other family members' needs and values.

Financial matters for most families are not safe areas to just jump into and blast away. It takes great effort and much listening to cultivate a **safe environment** where each family member can express his/her concerns. work on his/her own goals, take some responsibility for the family welfare and feel comfortable while doing all this!

As you continue on with these worksheets, remember their purpose is to help you and the others learn how to make statements so others can listen to you, respond to them, and help you make your own decisions. They give you and other family members the opportunity to tell each other what they think, feel and value. You would be surprised how many people are **afraid** to bring up certain issues with a spouse or parent.

One of the primary purposes of these worksheets is **to provide the opportunity to express oneself to other family members in a safe environment without sarcasm, fear of punishment, or discounting.**

The worksheets help to provide learned skills that may save you and your family members a great deal of wasted time, miscommunication and hostility.

It may feel different for you to follow these guidelines and use these worksheets, but the **purpose is to get everyone involved.** You may already know how to budget, spend, set goals, conduct board meetings, buy and sell in your name, invest, etc., but until **everyone** in your family learns all these skills, some of your responsibility goals are not yet completed. Encourage and teach other family members to use this book to understand their own financial values.

No one in the family should be left out of the process since everyone is a valued partner and an asset to the partnership.

Listening

1. Listen with your eyes and ears, not your mouth. Do not interrupt, make noises or blurt out anything. Be relaxed, you are **not going to be asked to agree or disagree.** Most family members just want to be heard.

2. When a family member is finished, **ask** if he/she is finished or if there is anything else. If not done, go back to step #1.

3. Wait a few seconds after he/she is done and ask "Is this what you meant to say?" Try to summarize their statements into <u>two</u> or <u>three</u> sentences. Keep it brief!

4. If he/she said you misunderstood, let him/her restate his/her ideas. Then summarize their ideas into two or three sentences again. If they say "Yes, you heard me correctly," you can now ask questions only for **clarification and understanding.** Asking sincere questions will help you get undefensive information and help your spouse realize you care about what he/she is saying.

5. Do not react to, renounce, argue about, agree or disagree with the person's remarks at this point. You are only **gathering information** in order to make a later decision, thus, you want people to **share their information without fear of judgment.**

Right now you will be practicing listening skills while fine-tuning your values, goals and financial self-inventory.

Worksheet Sixteen:
Listening Skills Practice Sheet

1. Ask your spouse to help you with this sheet whether or not he/she is doing the workbook. Ask him/her to read out loud each of the practice sentences A to G, one at a time. You will restate what you just heard before going to the next one.

2. If your spouse says you did not restate the statement accurately, then he/she needs to say to you, "you misunderstood me, please listen to my statement. Try again."

A. My financial goals are beginning to take shape in my life and I am going to write them all down.

B. I am a very complex person and I need a lot of understanding in my life.

C. I don't like it when you and the kids spend all the money and I don't know where it goes.

D. We live in a big brown house with blue shutters, a white door, and a two car garage. We have 4 children, 2 dogs, 3 cats and a bird.

E. I think you are a very controlling person when it comes to money.

F. I feel so good, worthy, and responsible when I can make my own financial choices.

G. The next car I buy is going to have a stick shift, get 40 mpg, have non-electric windows, and hold at least 6 people.

3. Practice again with H to M. Try to listen well the first time and notice which statements are easier to restate.

H. The red car would not start today and I have to have it fixed again at the dealership.

I. When there is no money left over at the end of the month, I get frustrated about how quickly it disappears.

J. The kids need to buy winter coats, boots, mittens, and hats. I will have to see if we have any money in the clothes budget.

K. I would like to work on a family budget with you next week on Monday night, 7 p.m. in the dining room.

L. The yard has such beautiful trees in it. There are 7 red maples, 4 blue spruce, and two 50-year old oak trees.

M. I am glad I am learning how to listen to and hear what other people are saying.

4. Remember you are practicing your listening skills. If your partner is doing the workbook, then he/she will request help from you at the appropriate time.

5. The next statements N to S are intended to be more controversial, but you are a more practiced listener now and you are not being asked to agree or disagree, just to listen and hear.

N. I need to tell you about how much work I do around the house. My day starts at 6 am with the baby and I don't get into bed until midnight without any breaks all day long. I am constantly interrupted even when I do sit down for five minutes. On top of that, I feel unappreciated.

O. My day at work was unbelievable. First the big meeting I worked so hard to prepare for, was rescheduled for next Thursday. Then the computer system had to shut down for 3 hours and we all became back-logged. By the time it was 5 p.m., I was still four hours behind in my work.

P. I have this really great idea for making money. I would like to sit down and figure out if there is any way we can invest in this real estate deal.

Q. I need to talk with you about our savings account. I would feel much more comfortable if I could have one in my own name. I always did when I was younger and I get a lot of self-worth from saving up my own money and then using it on my own choices.

R. Since we are in a marriage partnership, we need to set common financial goals so we both can work toward them. I hope you will do this financial workbook at the same time I do it.

S. Talking about finances with you can be a very difficult task. I have many ideas, dreams, and hopes that I would like to share with you. I need you to listen to my goals.

Worksheet Seventeen:
Gathering Information from Others

Another major aspect of communication skills is gathering information. You have just worked on your listening skills and now you can take it further by asking for more information about someone else's statements. Ask questions, but don't be argumentative. You are learning to provide an emotionally safe environment for all family members to share themselves with you. You are to be in the receiving mode when listening and asking questions.

Remember the communication process:

1) Listen reflectively,

2) Restate idea presented,

3) Sincerely ask questions to get more information, and

4) Listen to the answers without comment.

For statements A to G on the previous worksheet, what questions could you have asked to get more information? Some examples might be:

> *A. What financial goals are most important to you? Do you think about them a lot? Would you like some paper? Would you share them with me when you're done writing them down?*

B. *In what ways do you need a lot of support right now? What can I do to help you? What do you need from me?*

C. *Would you like it better if we tracked our spending so you know where the money goes? Would you like a monthly report? Do you need to have more input on what it is spent on? Are you frustrated with the way we are managing the money? Are you feeling appreciated enough for providing for us?*

D. *Does this big brown house have a fireplace, basement, or a swimming pool? Is it made out of brick or wood? Is it in a subdivision or in the country? Are the kids all boys, girls? What kind of dogs and cats do you have? Why do you have just one bird?*

E. *Do you think I am controlling you with the money? Could you give me an example? Has this been going on a long time?*

F. *Why does managing your own financial choices give you self-esteem? What kind of choices do you like to make?*

G. *Have you found a car like the one you want to buy? What is it called? Do you know how much it costs? What color would you make it?*

Go back to letters H to M on the previous worksheet and write down at least three questions you could ask for each of the statements.

H.

I.

J.

K.

L.

M.

Now ask your spouse to make the statements again for H to M, you restate the idea, then ask the questions you have just written down. Ask your spouse to make up answers to your questions.

Go to letters N through S and make up some sincere questions after your spouse makes a statement. Ask your spouse to make up the answers.

Worksheet Eighteen:
Your Listening Attitude

Answer these questions yes or no:

1. *Was it easy to restate all the statements?*

2. *Did you mess up on more than half of them?*

3. *Did you ever find yourself prejudging the speaker?*

4. *Was it easy to make up sincere questions?*

5. *If these had been your spouse's real life statements, would you have listened as well?*

6. *Do you usually give your opinion back to your spouse?*

7. *Do you usually ask questions to get more infor mation when your spouse brings up something to talk about?*

8. *Do you create a safe atmosphere for your spouse to talk about finances with you? How do you know?*

9. *Does your spouse feel comfortable bringing up financial topics with you? How do you know?*

10. *Are you willing to practice your listening skills whenever anyone in your family asks to speak with you on any subject?*

11. *Are you willing to set aside the opinion-giving habits in order to listen effectively?*

12. *Have you ever felt intimidated or put down after bringing up certain financial subjects with your spouse?*

13. *Do you think your spouse has ever felt intimidated or put down after bringing up certain financial subjects with you?*

14. *Have you ever noticed the subtle ways you might cut a family member off from talking with you?*

15. *If you knew it would always be safe to talk to your spouse about any financial subject, would you talk a lot more than you do now?*

16. *If you knew your spouse would always listen first, then ask questions to find out more information, would you talk with him/her about almost any financial subject?*

17. *Are you willing to take responsibility for yourself and practice these listening skills with your family members?*

Note:

It is easier to use these listening skills with strangers or acquaintances because you realize what they say will probably not impact your life. **It is more difficult to practice your listening skills with people who need your love and nurturing on a daily basis.** Yet your family members are the ones who need this consistency the most of all.

Worksheet Nineteen:
Tracking Communications with Others

This worksheet tracks the communication, appointments, and meetings you have with other family members. Use it to see how often your family members want to talk with you. Make notes to yourself about your listening abilities and your questions. Even if you have an informal talk about money with your spouse, jot down the date it occurred and the subject matter. You need to know whether or not you have financial conversations or how often they occur.

Date	*Person*	*Subject Matter*
1.		
2.		
3.		

4.

5.

6.

7.

8.

9.

10.

11.

12.

13.

14.

15.

Chapter Five:

Knowledge of Basic Financial Concepts

Step 1: READ

There is a wealth of financial knowledge all around us these days. There are financial seminars and books on every aspect of investing, real estate, bonds, retirement, budgeting, buying and selling anything, building your own business, etc.

This section contains a list of books which may be able to teach you about these financial topics. Put yourself on your own program to read one book every month for the next year. Read the book through quickly in the first few days. Then begin reading it again right away, but write down notes on a piece of 8x11 paper as you read it through the second time. Put these notes into your Reading Notes Section of your own financial notebook. Take notes for all the books. Worksheet #20 is used to track the actual books you read.

Continue with this book while participating in the reading program.

Worksheet Twenty: Reading Program

Title of Book/Author:

1. **Your Money Or Your Life** by Joe Dominquez and Vicki Robin

   Date completed:

2. **Kiplinger's 12 Steps to a Worry Free Retirement** by Daniel Kehrer

   Date completed:

3. **Financial Planning for Couples** by Adriane G. Berg

   Date completed:

5. **Fear of Finance** by Ann B. Diamond

   Date completed:

6. **Secure Your Future: Financial Planning at Any Age** by Chuck Tellalian and Walter Rosen

   Date completed:

7. **Taking Control of Your Financial Future**
by O'Hara and McLane

Date completed:

8. **The Millionaire Next Door**
by Thomas J. Stanley and Wm. D. Danko

Date completed:

9. **Simple Abundance**
by Sarah Ban Breathnatch

Date completed:

10. **Get a Financial Life** by Beth Kobliner

Date completed:

11. **The 9 Steps to Financial Freedom**
by Suze Orman

Date completed:

12. **Learn to Earn** by Peter Lynch and
John Rothchild

Date completed:

13. **The Totally Awesome Money Book for Kids and Their Parents** by Adriane G.
Berg and Arthur Berg Bochner

Date completed:

14. **Money and Marriage, Making It Work Together** by Steven Pybrum

Date completed:

Step 2:   BE DEBT-FREE

"Owe no man" anything is to become your motto. **Owe no money to any person, place or thing.** When you owe anything, then that person or thing or place can control you and your **choices** are severely restricted.

When you owe anything to anyone or an institution, it makes you dependent on that person, place, or thing because they can take something away from you. Make this **one of your major personal financial goals.** Many of the books on the reading list will show you how to reach this goal.

Each time you have to ask permission, get approval, or beg your spouse for the money to buy something or the time to do something, you are setting your marriage up for control and dependency. When you annually make choices for the amounts to be spent in different areas, annually agree to spending areas, and who is responsible for paying for them, then you are using money to empower each of you.

Most people need to learn how to assess their rights, choices, and responsibilities annually so the partnership can thrive, as well as each of you as individuals.

Use Worksheet #21 to list all your debts and put it in the **DEBT** section of your notebook. Write the goal to be **debt-free** on your 3"x5" index card. Carry it in your wallet where you keep your credit cards or cash money. Look at it often!

Worksheet Twenty-One:
My Debts

Anything and everything I have signed my name for or am responsible for paying.

Item	Amount Due	Date Paid
1.		
2.		
3.		
4.		
5.		

6.

7.

8.

9.

10.

11.

12.

Step 3:

KNOW WHERE YOUR MONEY GOES

Use these **eight** categories to write down all the money you spend over the next 30 days.

Housing:

Rent or house payments, utilities, telephone, property taxes, property, insurance, minor house repairs, furniture, appliances, decorating, lawn care, domestic help, remodeling, major improvements, landscaping

Transportation:

Bus, taxi, bicycle, motorcycle, auto payments or leases, insurance, gas, repairs, air travel, maintenance, licenses, taxes

Food:

Groceries, alcohol, cigarettes, dining out, takeout, school lunches

Kids:

Clothing, shoes, activities, lessons, camps, sports, child care help, day care, allowances, housework, pictures, rewards, gifts, birthdays, holidays

Family:

Week-end travel, week-long vacations, recreation, education, tuition, pets, hobbies, sports, basic clothing, work/school clothing, entertainment, gifts, dry cleaning, laundry, subscriptions, household supplies, personal items

Health Care:

Insurance, medical/dental visits, bills, drugs, medicine, supplies, counseling, testing, physical or psychological examinations

Money:

Contributions, family investments, personal investments, savings accounts, business investments, retirement funds, extra payments to pay off debts, professional advancement, business expenses, college funds, federal, state, or local income taxes, social security taxes

Miscellaneous: Anything else

Worksheet Twenty-Two:
30 Day Expense Tracking

---

1. Housing:

2. Transportation:

3. Food:

4. Kids:

5. Family:

6. Health Care:

7. Money:

8. Miscellaneous:

At the end of the 30 days, add up the expenses for each category and enter the total here.

Housing   _____

Transportation   _____

Food   _____

Kids   _____

Family   _____

Health Care   _____

Money   _____

Misc.   _____

Monthly Total   _____

Income Chart For This Past Month

Your Earned Income _____

Spouse's Earned Income _____

Investment Income _____

Gift Income _____

Business Income _____

Other _____

Monthly Total _____

Chapter Six:

Choices

This section on Choices may help you learn how:

1. To be aware of the many financial choices you already have,

2. To place a value on each one,

3. To reorganize and prioritize your spending areas,

4. To determine the amount to spend on each area,

5. To communicate your needs and choices to your spouse and yourself,

6. To become aware of your spouse's needs and choices, and

7. To prioritize your family's choices.

Take your time on the next worksheet. It is an important tool for defining your wants and needs, so be sincere and specific in your responses. Use the following numbers to indicate the level of priority to **you** personally.

1 = Eliminate from spending

2 = Low priority to me

3 = Average need or want to me

4 = High priority to me

5 = Must have, cannot live without

Rate the areas by **your** level of priority, not because of what another person thinks or wants you to do. This is your opportunity to prioritize your areas. Your spouse will be given the same opportunity to rate his/her choices. Be sure to mark the rating number that most reflects your level of importance.

Worksheet Twenty-Three:
Value Rating of Spending Areas

HOUSING: *#1-5 Value*

Rent or house payment

Utilities (gas, electric, water, sewer)

Telephone

Property Taxes

Property Insurance

Minor house repairs

Furniture/Appliances

Home decorating

Lawn care

Domestic help

Remodeling/major improvement

Landscaping

Other

TRANSPORTATION:
Taxi
Bus
Bicycle
Motorcycle
Auto payment or lease
Vehicle insurance
Gas
Maintenance, auto repairs
Air travel
Licenses
Taxes
Other

FOOD:
Groceries
Alcohol
Cigarettes
Dining out
Take-out
School lunches
Other

KIDS:

Clothing/shoes

Activities

Lessons

Camps

Sports

Babysitters

Full-time child care help

Day care

Allowances

Household work

Pictures

Rewards

Gifts

Birthdays

Holidays

Other

FAMILY:

Weekend travel

Week-long vacations

Recreation

Education

Tuition

Pets

Hobbies

Winter sports

Summer sports

Basic clothing

Work/school clothing

Entertainment

Gifts (Christmas, B-day, baby, grad, weddings)

Dry cleaning

Laundry

Subscriptions

Household supplies

Personal items

Other

HEALTH CARE:

Insurance

Medical visits

Dental visits

Drugs

Medicine

Supplies

Counseling

Testing

Physical Examinations

Psychological Examinations

Medical bills

Other

MONEY:

Contributions/charity

Personal investments

Family investments

Savings account

Business investments

Retirement funds

Extra payments to pay off debts

Professional advancement

Business expenses

College funds

Federal, state, or local income taxes

Social Security taxes

Other

MISC.:

Other

Other

Other

Other

TOTAL # WITH A "5" RATING _____

TOTAL # WITH A "4" RATING _____

TOTAL # WITH A "3" RATING _____

TOTAL # WITH A "2" RATING _____

TOTAL # WITH A "1" RATING _____

You are now ready to request an appointment with your spouse. If he/she is working through the book, then wait for him/her to finish the value rating worksheet before continuing with the next paragraph. If not, skip to step 4.

This appointment will help you determine how close your spending choices are. Again, the ground rules for communicating are simply:

1. listen without giving any rebuttal,

2. state your ratings without any explanations, then,

3. read the following statement out loud:

"I am looking forward to sharing my spending choices and priorities with you. We will be compiling our choices onto lists together and it may take some time. I will not attempt to change your ratings and I'd appreciate it if you would accept mine as stated. This is probably the first time we have done this together, so we may be in for some surprises. Remember, please don't make any put-down statements about my choices and I'll be respectful of your choices, too."

4. If your spouse is <u>not</u> doing the workbook, then read the following statement out loud to him/her:

"I have some financial information about myself which I would like to share with you. I have compiled a list of spending areas and rated them according to my own preferences. I would really like you to know what is important to me. I'd also like to learn about your spending choices, too, when you're ready to share that information with me. Anyway, thanks for taking the time to hear about my financial choices."

5. Share the information from Worksheet 23 with your spouse/fiance.

Worksheet Twenty-Four:
Value Rating Summary

Do this worksheet together, but each of you writes in the information on his/her own worksheet as you go along together.

*1. List all spending items with a "5" or "4" rating from **both** of you.*

a.

b.

c.

d.

e.

f.

g.

h.

i.

j.

k.

*2. List all spending items with a "3" rating from
both of you.*

a.

b.

c.

d.

*3. List all spending areas with a "2" rating from
both of you.*

a.

b.

c.

d.

e.

f.

g.

4. *List all spending areas with a "1" rating from* **both** *of you.*

a.

b.

c.

d.

e.

f.

g.

h.

5. *List the rest of your own ratings starting with 5's:*

a.

b.

c.

6. List the rest of your spouse's ratings starting with the 5's:

a.

b.

c.

Write all of your own 5 and 4 ratings on one side of a 3x5 card and all your spouse's 5 and 4 ratings on the other side. Each time you look at your priorities, take a look at your spouse's, too.

Ask yourself these questions, **"Am I encouraging myself to reach these goals with or without my spouse's help? Am I encouraging my spouse to reach for his/her goals without requiring my approval?"**

Once the spending choices have been prioritized, go back and put a dollar amount next to each one. Write in the **minimum** amount you would be willing to spend for the expense per month.

Your spouse should do this separately on his/her own worksheet #24. Do not try to manipulate or adjust your figures to offset your spouse's amounts. Just concentrate on being honest in your amounts and do not analyze what anyone else might be doing.

Compare your amounts with your spouse's amounts. In the margin, write in the amount which is half way between your dollar value and his/her dollar value. Circle this amount and continue doing it all the way through #6.

Note:

Practice your listening skills. All you need to do is follow the instructions. **You are not to discuss, defend, or argue about either of your amounts.** Each one of you is entitled to his/her own opinion. You are still just gathering and sharing information to make a later decision. **You have a lot more knowledge and information to gather before you can make any intelligent decisions,** so please keep your opinions about your spouse's choices to yourself.

The objectives of this worksheet are 1) to help you list your spending priorities, and 2) to show you how your spouse and family may have very specific needs and wants of their own.

Put these two worksheets in your own notebook under the **CHOICE** section.

Worksheet Twenty-Five:
Choices in Different Situations

Write in the words "**possible**" or "**not possible**" after each sentence.

A. Let's say I bring home $5000/month and my spouse does not earn income, I could .....

1. Spend it all on my choices and give no one else access to my money unless I give it.

2. Spend it on my choices, but give everyone an allowance of spending money.

3. Give it all to my spouse to pay bills and keep an allowance for myself.

4. Designate a certain amount to common expenses and let my spouse pay those bills.

5. Pay a certain amount to my spouse for being the children's primary caretaker and then he/she pays a certain portion of the bills.

6. Pay a certain amount to my spouse for taking care of the other family responsibilities like cooking, cleaning, shopping, etc. and then he/she pays a certain portion of the bills.

7. Pay my spouse half of my income and we then pay the common family bills evenly. Whatever is left over, we each can spend on our individual choices.

8. Write in your best idea:

B. Let's say I bring home $4000/month and my spouse brings home $1000/month, I could ....

1. Spend my money only on my own choices.

2. Agree to common living expenses and pay for 4/5's of them.

3. Pay my spouse for being the primary caretaker of the kids.

4. Pay my spouse for being the primary caretaker of other family responsibilities like cooking, cleaning, shopping, etc.

5. Only pay half of the expenses since I'm paying my spouse for childcare or other work.

6. Whatever I have left over, I could spend on my individual choices and so could my spouse.

7. Agree to a family checking account, an individual one for myself, and one for my spouse.

8. Pay someone else to do the domestic chores and I would pay 4/5's of the expense.

9. Pay someone else to be the primary child raiser and I would pay 4/5's of the expense.

10. Write in your best idea for these conditions:

C. Answer yes or no. Let's say I go to graduate school for three years, we have no kids, and my spouse is the only one working to support both of us during that time.

1. Do I have the right to make any financial deci-sions? Half of the financial decisions?

2. Do I get an allowance to spend on whatever I want?

3. Am I willing to do all the housework? Half of it?

4. When I finish school and go to work, will our financial income increase?

5. Do I get to make all the financial decisions then?

6. Am I willing to let my spouse go to school for the next three years while I support him/her?

7. After graduation, is my spouse now entitled to half of my paycheck since he/she worked to put me through school? If yes, for how long? If no, why not?

8. Am I valuing my spouse for directly contributing to my achievements?

9. If I were not married, how much money would I have borrowed in order to go to school without working?

10. Would you be willing to pay this amount to your spouse for enabling you to concentrate just on your studies? If yes, how much over the next three years? If no, why not?

11. Write in your best idea for these conditions:

D. Answer yes or no. Let's say my husband and I have started a business together with $30,000 from our savings account. He has a 50 hr/week job earning about $40,000/year. I work for our business about thirty hours each week, but do most all the child care, shopping, and housework, too.

1. Do I have the right to make up all the financial decisions of the new business? Half of them?

2. Do I have the right to decide what to do with the profits and the losses?

3. If I am doing all the work for the business, should my husband receive half of the profits and half of the losses?

4. Should I pay myself first before dispensing any profits?

5. If I have done all the work and the business is making $50,000/year after taxes and expenses, do I split it with my husband?

6. What if he quits his job and our only income is from this business? Should he do most of the child care, shopping, and housework? Should he get to make half of the financial decisions regarding the business now?

7. Would you want him to quit his job? Would you be willing to buy him out?

8.   Write in your best idea for these conditions:

E. Answer yes or no. Let's say in a long term marriage, over ten years, do you think:

1. Both partners should put everything they earn into one checkbook and then pay family expenses from it?

2. The partner who receives a paycheck should pay the one who doesn't work outside the home?

3. The partner who earns more, should pay more on the common household bills?

4. The partner who brings home a paycheck should be able to make investments and the other one is not given the choice?

5. Your partner should have to get approval from you for food, clothing, or regular household purchases?

6. All acquired assets during the marriage are morally half your spouse's? Legally half your spouse's?

7. If he/she never worked outside the home for the last ten years, is half of everything still his/hers?

8. Should the husband be the main financial provider through-out the marriage?

9. Should the wife be the main financial provider through-out the marriage?

10. If you are a corporate wife for your husband's job, is this essentially a career?

11. If you are a corporate husband for your wife's job, is this essentially a career?

12. Write in your best ideas:

F. Answer yes or no. Let's say your spouse has retired and you are still working outside the home, do you think ...

1. The working spouse should pay the retired spouse for doing the housework?

2. The retired spouse should cook, clean, make purchases, and take care of the home?

3. The retired spouse can do whatever he/she wants because of retirement?

4. The working spouse now gets to decide where the earned income goes?

5. The retired spouse gets to decide how the retirement annuity, social security, or pension plans get to be spent or allocated?

6. Write in your best ideas for these conditions:

G. Answer yes or no. Let's say you have remarried someone with as demanding and highly paid job as your own. Both of you are making over $100,000 per year, but you are also responsible for child and spousal support payments of $3500/month for your first marriage. Do you think ...

1. Both partners should put all income into a family checking account to pay bills?

2. Both partners should seek legal and financial advice before remarriage?

3. Both partners should have a pre-nuptial agreement regarding assets and finances?

4. Monthly financial meetings are still important to set common goals?

5. The non-parental spouse should have to contribute to your child or spousal support payments?

6. Both partners should maintain separate checkbooks and pay equally for common household expenses?

7. You should be paid to take care of your spouse's children during his/her parenting time?

8. In this case, what would your answers be if you both made $20,000 a year, with support payments of $1000/month?

9. Write in your best ideas for these conditions:

H. Answer yes or no. Let's say your spouse recently inherited $90,000 from a distant relative. Do
you think...

*1. It is his/her money to spend, account for, invest,
waste, or give away?*

*2. It should be put in the family account to be used
for family bills?*

*3. It should be allocated for certain items only after
a family decision?*

*4. It should be used to pay off all bills of family
members and then whatever is left over, the inheritor
gets to spend as he/she wishes.*

*5. It is none of your business what your spouse does
with the inheritance?*

6. Describe your best ideas:

*7. Would your answers be different if your spouse
inherited $1000.00 instead of $90,000? How?*

I. Answer yes or no. Let's say your spouse recently won $90,000 in a state lottery. Do you think...

1. It is his/her money to spend, account for, invest, waste, or give away?

2. It should be put in the family account to be used for family bills?

3. It should be allocated for certain items only after a family decision?

4. It should be used to pay off all bills of family members and then whatever is left over, the winner gets to spend as he/she wishes.

5. It is none of your business what your spouse does with the prize money?

6. Describe your best ideas:

7. Would your answers be different if your spouse recently won $1000.00 instead of $90,000?

J. Answer yes or no. Let's say I have a job making $30,000 per year. I marry someone with two small children and want a child of our own. My new spouse stays at home. I could..

1. Spend it all on my choices and give no one else access to my money unless I give it.

2. Spend it on my choices, but give everyone an allowance of spending money.

3. Give it all to my spouse to pay bills and keep an allowance for myself.

4. Designate a certain amount to common expenses and let my spouse pay those bills.

5. Pay a certain amount to my spouse for being the primary child raiser and then he/she pays a certain portion of the bills.

6. Pay a certain amount to my spouse for taking care of the other family responsibilities like cooking, cleaning, shopping, etc. and then he/she pays a certain portion of the bills.

7. Pay my spouse half of my income and we then pay the common family bills evenly. Whatever is left over, we each can spend on our individual choices.

8. Pay for all the support of the two children.

9. Write in your best idea:

K. Write in your own opinion:

1. What would you do with your time if you were laid off from your job, but your spouse is still working?

2. What would you do with your time if you married someone who is independently wealthy?

3. What would you do with your time if you were independently wealthy and married someone who was not?

4. If your spouse developed a gambling problem, what would you do about it? How would you protect your assets from being used?

5. If your spouse developed an alcohol problem and could not work, what would you do about it?

6. *Before you marry, will you be able to ask your potential partner to see his/her recent financial records and show your records to him/her?*

7. *Before you marry, would you be able to find out what your potential partner's credit rating is and show your credit rating to him/her?*

8. *Before you marry, would you be able to ask for verification on all debts and income for the potential partner and verify your debts and income to him/her?*

9. *If you own property or a house before you marry, should your new spouse buy half interest in the assets? Or should you keep them in your name only?*

10. *Before you marry, would you be able to find out if your potential partner is involved in any lawsuits, accidents, severe illness, large medical expenses, care of other dependents, or possible bankruptcy? Are you willing to share your information on these topics with him/her?*

11. What is your current method of paying expenses and depositing income?

- *Joint checking*

- *Separate checking*

- *Savings account*

- *Combination savings and checking*

- *Allowance*

- *Sugar bowl method*

- *Envelopes for each budget area*

- *Other*

12. Indicate which person:

- *Pays the bills*

- *Sorts the mail*

- *Files the receipts*

- *Balances the checkbook*

- *Makes deposits and withdrawals*

- *Makes most of the financial decisions*

- *Budgets the income*

L. How would you handle the finances if you were sharing a house with several people who just graduated from college?

1. Would you still have financial meetings?

2. Would you divide up the common expenses by person or by income?

3. Would one person be responsible for paying common bills?

4. How would you know if that person is actually paying them on time?

5. Would you consider buying a house with several friends?

6. What would you do if one of them lost his/her job and could not pay common expenses?

7. Any other ideas?

M. Answer yes or no. Do you like...

1. To be controlled? To control others?

2. To have to get approval for any kind of purchase? To have to give approval for purchases?

3. The freedom to make your own decisions? To encourage others to make their own decisions?

4. To be fair in your dealings with others? To have others be fair with you?

5. To know what other family members do with their own money? To have other family members check on your purchases?

6. To have the final say on common family purchases? To have someone else have the final say on common family purchases?

7. To have others ask you for money? To have to ask others for money?

8. Do you think your spouse should have the final say over the family budget? You?

9. *Would you like to be able to talk about these value choices with your spouse? Would he/she like to be able to talk with you?*

10. *Would this worksheet start a lot of arguments? Would you really like to know what your spouse thinks? Would you really like to be able to tell your spouse what you think?*

11. *How do you react when your spouse disagrees with you? Anger, withdrawal, retaliation, or understanding? How does your spouse react when you disagree?*

N.   Answer these questions yes or no.

1. Does your spouse/potential partner tell you what his/her monthly income is?

2. Have you ever shown your paystubs to your spouse/potential partner?

3. Are you hesitant to ask your spouse/potential partner how much money he/she makes each month?

4. Are you hesitant to tell your spouse/potential partner how much money you make each month?

5. Are you hesitant to ask your spouse/potential partner how much money he/she spends each month?

6. Are you hesitant to tell your spouse/potential partner how much money you spend each month?

7. Have you ever prioritized your spending goals together?

8. Do you ever have regular financial meetings with each other?

9. Are you willing to share the answers from this worksheet with your spouse/potential partner?

10. If no, set a date in six months to review this worksheet and see if you can do it then.

11. If yes, show him/her respect by making this statement before sharing the answers:

"Thanks for having the courage to listen to my answers to these hard questions. You might not like the answers because they could initially create conflict. I want to share my information with you and receive your information from you. I respect your willingness to listen to me. I am trying to learn whether or not we have created a safe environment to express our concerns to each other. You need to know what I honestly think about certain situations. You need to be able to make your own decisions based on what I need and am able to give to you, just as I need to know what you honestly think about certain situations."

Give him/her this worksheet to read.

Worksheet Twenty-Six:
High Priority Family Choices

A. List all the choices with a 5 or 4 rating which directly **benefit any two or more family members** from WS 23. Write in the circled dollar amount.

1.

2.

3.

4.

5.

6.

7.

8.

9.

10.

11.

12.

13.

14.

15.

16.

17.

18.

19.

20.

21.

22.

23.

24.

25.

26.

27.

28.

29.

30.

Total Monthly Amount =_____

*B. List all the choices with a 5 or 4 rating which benefit only **you**. Write in the circled dollar amount.*

1.

2.

3.

4.

5.

6.

7.

8.

*Total Monthly Amount =*_____

C. List all the choices with a 5 or 4 rating which benefit only your spouse. Write in the circled dollar amount.

1.

2.

3.

4.

5.

6.

7.

8.

*Total Monthly Amount =*_____

D. List all the choices with a 5 or 4 rating which benefit only one child or other dependent. Write in the circled amount.

1.

2.

3.

4.

5.

6.

7.

8.

*Total Monthly Amount =*_____

E. Same for second child or dependent:

1.

2.

3.

4.

5.

6.

7.

8.

*Total Monthly Amount =*_____

F. Same for third child or dependent:

1.

2.

3.

4.

5.

6.

7.

8.

*Total Monthly Amount =*_____

G. List the total amounts here:

Your family total _____

Your own total _____

Your spouse's total _____

Child _____

Child _____

Child _____

Other Dependent _____

High Priority

Spending Choices _____

H. Compare your total amounts to your spouses. Are you and your spouse in spending proximity of each other's totals?

Worksheet Twenty-Seven:
Choices for Sharing Income

---

*A. My total **gross** monthly income is:*

*B. I would like to designate these amounts of **my** income to these categories:*

My Choices

Spouse's Choices

Family Choices

*C. I would like to dispense the money for the **common family choices** in this way:*

D. I would like to dispense the money for my **spouse's choices** *in this way:*

E. I would like to dispense the money for **my choices** *in this way:*

F. I would like the money to be **accounted** *for in this way:*

Family Expenses:

My Expenses:

Spouse's Expenses:

Children's Expenses:

Other Dependents:

The purpose of this worksheet is for you to honestly state how much of your income you would intend to divert to each of these three areas and how you plan to do it. This is very important information to share with your spouse.

At this time, keep this worksheet to yourself until you are instructed to use it again.

Note:

If you have a spouse who works in the home, but is not paid by you or anyone else, he/she may opt to take the responsibility of asking you for money, getting a job or starting a business in order to have money to spend on his/her choices. Or he/she may decide it is too difficult to live with someone who does not share his/her money, especially if the partner is contributing to the overall welfare of the family through child care or housework.

There are no specific formulas to help you decide whether or not your situation is fair. Only you can know if you have **choices,** can take **responsibilities,** and are gaining financial **knowledge** in your partnership.

If your over-all goal is to have each family member be financially self-sufficient and capable, then you will design a financial system for your family which offers choice, rights, and responsibility to each member without any one person's control or domination of another.

Worksheet Twenty-Eight:
Choices for Non-Wage Workers

This is to be completed by spouses who do not work outside the home or earn small amounts of money compared to the spouse who brings in much larger amounts.

1. Since I provide the major portion of the child care and home care, I would like to receive this amount of money each month:

2. I would divide the income coming to me this way:

My Choices

Family Choices

Spouse's

3. I would pay for my choices in this way:

4. I would pay for the family choices in this way:

5. I would pay for my spouse's choices by:

6. I am willing to account for this money by doing:

Family Expenses:

My Expenses:

Spouse's Expenses:

Others:

This might be a very difficult exercise for you to complete if you have never asked to be paid for your housework or childcare. The purpose of this exercise is not for you to threaten your spouse with your independence, but to gain choices, responsibility, and value for your contribution to the family welfare. This exercise could be totally rejected and you obviously have no way of making your spouse pay you. But remember, you need the opportunity to make choices and to be responsible for part of the financial well-being of the family as much as your spouse does.

It is crucial to your development as a whole person to be recognized by your spouse as contributing to the overall welfare of the family. One of the ways to recognize this contribution you make, is to have your spouse pay you for it each time he/she gets paid.

In the overall plan, the money may still be spent on the same choices as before, but the responsibility will be shared and managed by each adult. If you have an alternative idea, write it here:

Notes:

Chapter Seven:

Responsibilities

The main objective of the Responsibilies chapter is to help you learn what your financial responsibilities are in your family. Your **first** responsibility is to **respect** the rights, choices, and responsibilities of **your partner** and **yourself.**

Your **second** responsibility in the partnership of marriage is to establish an environment where healthy **communication and decision-making is possible for all family members.**

The worksheets in this chapter are designed to help the partners make financial decisions in a business-like manner and to be able to present their ideas and decisions to each other in a safe environment.

In this section, you may also take the responsibility of learning how to set annual budgets, to allocate money to the different categories, to track your spending, to argue constructively for your point of view, to conduct a financial meeting with your spouse or family, and to initiate other responsibilities.

In previous chapters, you began to understand your own values and choices regarding money. Hopefully, you listened to your spouse's values and choices regarding money, as well.

Now we are going to put it all together by learning to use the **Financial Concerns Worksheet, Family Idea Worksheet, Family Decision Worksheet,** and **Family Financial Agenda Worksheet.**

In order to promote your number one and two financial responsibilities, you need to follow these guidelines:

1. For one full year, it is your own responsibility to conduct **monthly** financial meetings with your spouse (whether or not he/she chooses to participate in this book), to share information, to seek information, and to make decisions based on the information gathered. Do not discuss any financial matters outside the context of this meeting. All ideas, disagreements, and decisions need to be brought up at these meetings on a **specific worksheet.** Set up a specific time and day for each month to hold these meetings and enter them in your calendar now.

2. Another one of your responsibilities is to conduct the meeting as if you were in a business setting where the board members have **equal responsibility for deciding the welfare of the partnership.** You will **rotate** the chair position each month between two adults.

3. Your final responsibility is to use specific worksheets at the financial meetings for communicating all ideas, problems, and decisions for at least a year. if you are just beginning to have meetings, you may choose to have them once/week until you are caught up.

4. Fill out the Financial Concerns Worksheet for every concern, problem or disagreement you want to bring up with your spouse.

When you disagree with any statement or conclusion your spouse has made through his/her own worksheets or in a conversation, then fill out a **Concerns** worksheet to use for communicating your concerns at the next weekly family meeting. Do not discuss it ahead of time. Fill out a different one for each main disagreement. You may not complain or plan revenge for any statement your spouse may have made.

You must use the Concerns Worksheet to communicate your dissatisfaction on any financial subject. You may have many of these worksheets for your first few meetings.

5. When you need to discuss **positive** family priorities or choices, you should use the **Family Idea Worksheet** to lead the partnership through a useful discussion on any topic you think is important. Do not use this sheet for making complaints or for reversing prior decisions. This worksheet is used for the **communication of positive ideas and choices.**

6. The **Family Decision Worksheet** is used at your family meetings to actually vote on a concern or an idea presented through the other two worksheets. The Decision Worksheet is used to **summarize the decision agreed upon by the couple or by the family.**

7. The **Financial Meeting Agenda Worksheet** contains the **format for conducting** the family financial meetings. It should be followed and completed by the person conducting the meeting. Remember, this position is to be **rotated** every month so each adult has the responsibility for conducting these partnership meetings.

The format of the financial meetings is to be used each time because it may help to provide a safe environment to discuss important financial topics, whether you are working on the annual budget or are disagreeing with a position your spouse has taken.

Please photocopy these worksheets so each family member has access to as many as he/she needs. Sign here after you have read the information regarding these worksheets.

I agree to take the responsibility for using these family meeting worksheets on a monthly basis for a period of one full year, even if no one else in my family chooses to do the same.

Signed _____

Date   _____

Worksheet Twenty-Nine:
Financial Concern/Problems

Complete each sentence on this sheet and bring it with you to the next family financial meeting. Tell the person conducting the meeting how many concern worksheets you have to discuss. Read your statements aloud to the other people present.

1. *I think there is a problem with ...*

2. *It is a concern to me because ....*

3. *"Did you hear what I said? Please restate my concern in your own words."*

4. *I think it could be resolved by doing ...*

5. *Do you have any feedback for me?*

6. Read this aloud:

"Thank you for listening to my concern. If it is important enough to me to have this resolved by our family, then I will follow through and ask a vote on some action by using the family decision worksheet. Thanks for listening to my concerns."

Note:

Now that you have received some feedback from other family members, you need to decide if the problem is enough of a concern to actually take action on. If it is something you can handle on your own and does not involve other family members, then take care of it. If it is something that needs to go through the partnership process, then fill out a decision worksheet before the next family meeting.

Remember, this sheet is **used to introduce your concern** to other family members. It is more important for you to be able **to present it to them than it is to have them agree with you.** You are not asking for agreement or disagreement at this point.

Put this in the Family Notebook under the "Concerns" section after presenting it at the family meeting.

Worksheet Thirty:
Family Financial Ideas

Complete the first three sentences before the family meeting. Tell the person conducting the meeting that you would like to be put on the agenda for discussion of an "idea" worksheet.

1. I would like to talk about the idea of ..

2. It is important to me because ....

3. It could be implemented by doing ....

4. Did you hear what my idea was? (Ask each member to restate).

5. Would you give me some initial feedback on the idea:

6. Read this statement out loud:

"Thank you for listening and giving me some feedback on this idea. If I think it is valuable enough to pursue, then I will bring it to a vote on a family decision worksheet. Otherwise, I might just handle it on my own. Thanks for listening."

Note:

If this is an important idea to you and it needs to go through the family, then solidify your ideas and put them on a family decision worksheet before the next family meeting. If the idea is something you can pursue on your own, go for it. Put this worksheet in the Family Notebook under the "Ideas" section.

Worksheet Thirty-One: Family Decisions

This worksheet is a request to take specific action regarding a concern, an idea, or a prior decision which affects the family.

Complete numbers 1 to 6 before presenting this worksheet at a family meeting. Tell the person conducting the meeting that you have a Decisions Worksheet to put on the agenda.

1. It is very important to me to ... (implement, change, discontinue, etc.)

2. I brought this up as an idea or concern on _____ at a family meeting to get your initial feedback and to introduce it.

3. My main reasons/benefits for wanting this (change, idea, etc.) are:

a.

b.

c.

d.

4. It could be specifically implemented by doing:

a.

b.

c.

d.

5. Each one of us would have these responsibilities, choices, and rights by implementing this decision:

Me

Spouse

Child

6. In summary, I would just like to restate what I am asking for a vote on:

7. After reading numbers 1 to 6 out loud at the meeting, have an informal discussion with input from each family member. Each one gets to speak once before anyone gets a second turn. Try to limit total discussion to 10 minutes. Each person listens respectfully as the others give their opinions.

8. Ask members if they are ready for a vote on the statement in #6. If the majority say "not ready" then table the vote to the next meeting.

Note:

A family decision can only be tabled once. At the next meeting, a vote should be taken either supporting the decision or against it. These family decisions are **not** to be prolonged for any reason.

9. If the majority answered, "Yes, ready to vote," then:

a. repeat the issue to be voted on from #6

b. discuss any minor changes for implementation

c. take a vote to see if the majority votes for the proposal or against it.

10. Vote Tally:

My vote:

Spouse's vote:

Children's votes (if applicable):

Note:

You may need to negotiate until a reasonable agreement can be worked out.

Put this worksheet in the Decisions section of the Family Financial Notebook after the vote.

Worksheet Thirty-Two:
Financial Meeting Agenda

Date: *Time:*

Location:

Members Present:

I. Make a general statement of safety and security for all opinions, suggestions, and worksheets which will be given today.

II. Discussion of **Treasurer's Report** *(monthly or annual family budget sheets)*

III. Old Business:

A. Discussion of financial **Decision worksheets** *from:*

1.

2.

3.

B. Votes taken on **Decision worksheets:**

1.

2.

3.

IV. New Business:

*A. Discussion of new financial **Concerns** worksheets from:*

1.

2.

*B. Discussion of new financial **Idea** worksheets from:*

1.

2.

*C. Discussion of new **Decision** worksheets:*

1.

2.

D. Worksheets to be tabled until the next meeting:

1.

2.

V. Closing statement: Thank each person for input and how you look forward to the next meeting for sharing more information.

Note:

This format is designed to help the family stay on track during financial meetings and to introduce basic business meeting etiquette. This does not have to be a formal process, but until **everyone is comfortable bringing up concerns, making decisions, conducting meetings, and introducing ideas, all in a non-hostile environment,** then your family may need to use this kind of structure for a couple of years.

Put this in the **Family** Financial Notebook after each meeting under the Family Meeting section.

Worksheet Thirty-Three: Annual Family Budget

1. Prepare these sheets on your own.

2. Use a separate sheet for **each** month.

3. Write in your own **categories** and budgeted **amounts** from your value rating worksheet.

4. Use a blank worksheet to add up and summarize your 12 budget sheets as your **Annual Family Budget.**

5. Combine your annual budget with your spouse's annual budget onto a new sheet now. Work until you have agreed upon amounts for every category.

6. This is a partnership agreement which you both are responsible for managing during the next year. You will be transferring this information to monthly tracking sheets, so put this combined worksheet in the Annual Budget section. Put your own worksheets in your notebook under the Choices section.

7. This annual budget should be agreed upon by December 1 of every year, prior to its implementation on January 1 of the new year.

8. Both partners sign the annual budget worksheet which they have agreed to use for the upcoming year.

9. After the new year begins, either partner may bring up ideas, changes, or conflicts with the set amounts by using the worksheets given for the family meetings. Any changes would have to be agreed upon at a Family Financial Meeting using the worksheets.

ANNUAL BUDGET FOR THE YEAR:

Budgeted Amount

HOUSING: _____

TRANSPORTATION: _____

FOOD: _____

KIDS: _____

FAMILY: _____

HEALTH CARE: _____

MONEY: _____

MISC: _____

Worksheet Thirty-Four:
Who is Responsible?

1. Take the total amounts from your signed annual budget and indicate what amount will be put in each account, when, and by whom.

2. Complete this worksheet within two weeks after the annual budget is signed.

3. Decide which partner will manage the Family Account for this upcoming year. It is a job which should be rotated each year.

4. Sign this worksheet after completion.

5. Even if you do not actually open up separate checking accounts for you and your spouse, it is very important to receive your money for your own choices without having to **ask** anyone else for it. Once the categories and amounts are set up in the budget, the money should be disbursed without having to ask anyone for approval or asking for it to be put in the account.

6. Put this worksheet in the **Annual Budget section of the Family Notebook.**

Account:	_Family_	_Mine_	_Spouse's_

HOUSING:

Amount:

When:

By Whom:

TRANSPORTATION:

Amount:

When:

By Whom:

FOOD:

Amount:

When:

By Whom:

KIDS:

Amount:

When:

By Whom:

Account:	_Family_	_Mine_	_Spouse's_

FAMILY:

Amount:

When:

By Whom:

HEALTH CARE:

Amount:

When:

By Whom:

MONEY:

Amount:

When:

By Whom:

MISC:

Amount:

When:

By Whom:

Signed _____

Signed _____

Date _____

Worksheet Thirty-Five:
Tracking your Monthly Expenses

In order to track your **family** expenses on a daily basis, each family member takes certain responsibilities for recording data. Your family members should track their expenses on a daily basis. This information is to be compiled and shared at the financial meetings.

1. Give each person in the family a small notebook to record cash expenses, no matter how minor. At the end of each week, he/she transfers the information from his/her **notebook** to the monthly family tracking sheet which is posted for **all to use and see.**

2. At the end of the month, the partner responsible for managing the family accounts and family charge cards, tallies the category amounts and puts them on the monthly tracking sheet for all to see and review at any time. It is important to break down and categorize the amounts from the monthly charge statement in order to get an accurate view of spending, or it may be easier to write down/track the charges as they occur and then doublecheck the amounts *when the statements come in.*

3. This tracking sheet is used as the **Treasurer's Report** for the monthly review. It is to be put in the **family** notebook after the meeting.

4. A new blank tracking sheet is put in a common location (such as, on the refrigerator) for the family to use for the new month.

5. In order to custom design your own monthly tracking sheets for all twelve months, use accounting paper with columns across the top. Take the spending categories from your budget worksheet and insert them on the lines going down the left side of the page.

6. Make up a **separate sheet for all twelve months** and insert all the categories which will come up in that month. For example, if you pay your auto insurance twice a year, you would add that category to the transportation section for those months. You are custom-designing your own budget book for the family to use, based on the annual budget amounts, choices and categories you have selected.

7. As you manage your own **personal** spending choices, you may choose to custom-design your own budget sheets to track your monthly spending. These do not need to be shared at any family financial meeting unless you choose to show them. Put them in your personal notebook.

8. The monthly tracking/budget sheet for the **common family expenses** needs to be on a combined sheet for all to see at anytime.

9. I use the computer program, **Quicken™**, for our family finances. I write down the cash expenses in my daily calendar book as they occur and then transfer them to the **Quicken™** program about once a week. All check payments are produced through this program, whether hand-written or laser-printed,

so those expenses are automatically transferred to categories by **Quicken™**.

10. I entered my own spending categories when I first started using the computerized program. **Quicken™** allows me to customize all the budgeted categories and then add family names to further categorize spending. When I pay a health care bill for a son, for example, the program tracks the budget category, the provider of service, the amount paid and which family member the amount benefited.

Example

Pay to: _Provider of Service_ _____

Amount: _____

Budget Category: _____

For whom: _____

(This information shows up on many reports)

11. When I receive a charge card statement, the program allows me to take each line item and categorize it with the amount. Then when I print out reports, the individual charge shows up in the proper category, whether groceries, gas, clothing, or a dinner at a restaurant and whether or not it was for a specific family member.

12. When I pay by check, the program automatically records the proper category, and then each expense shows up on the reports in the correct spending area. I print out a monthly "itemized spending" report which shows all spending, whether by cash, check, or charge.

13. My family finance file is titled "Family 99,"

my business financial file is titled "FLP 99," the church accounting which I do is titled "Church 99," etc. Quicken™ allows you to open a separate file for each business or organization or family which needs accounting. As the year ends, I change the title to indicate the new year. I update the spending categories each year, as well, and customize them however they best serve my family or organization.

14. Whether you track your spending by hand or computer, you will end up with actual amounts spent in each category each month. Your family needs this information on a monthly basis.

15. Example of Monthly Tracking Sheet: This may be for the month of June. You enter the spending categories down the left side for which you anticipate paying expenses.

Housing:	*Budgeted*	*Actual*
Rent		
Utilities		
Telephone		
Lawn Care		
Transportation:		
Auto payment		
Gas		
Insurance		
Repairs		

Food:	_Budgeted_	_Actual_
Groceries	_____	_____
Take Out	_____	_____
School Lunches	_____	_____

Kids:		
Clothing/Shoes	_____	_____
Activities	_____	_____
Allowances	_____	_____
Child Care	_____	_____

Family:		
Pets	_____	_____
Hobbies	_____	_____
Work Clothes	_____	_____
Entertainment	_____	_____
Gifts	_____	_____
Subscriptions	_____	_____

Health Care:		
Insurance	_____	_____
Medical bills	_____	_____
Medicine	_____	_____
Supplies	_____	_____

Money:		
Contributions	_____	_____
Retirement Account	_____	_____
College Fund	_____	_____
Spending money/allowances	_____	_____
Extra payments on loans	_____	_____

Miscellaneous:		
	_____	_____

ORDER FORM

This book is a valuable tool for all married couples and we encourage you to order copies for other family members and friends. Each couple should have a working copy of this book containing their own personal financial information and worksheets.

Telephone orders: 616-348-1813
Fax orders: 616-348-0756
Mail orders: Torch Lake Publishing
                  P.O. Box R
                  Petoskey, MI   49770-0918 USA

Please print your name and address:

Name _____

Address _____

City _____ State ___ Zip _____

Telephone Number _____

_____ Quantity of books   @ $15.95:   _____

        Sales tax for Michigan orders @ 6%   _____

        Shipping cost   3.05
                                             _____

                              TOTAL   _____

Payment: ___ Check enclosed   ___ Credit card

Type of Card: ☐ Visa   ☐ Mastercard

Name on card: _____

Card number: _____ Expires: _____

Authorizing signature: _____